THE PERFECT FUCKING LIFE

Jason Lee Morrison

ISBN: 978-1-951503-68-0 (Hardcover)
ISBN: 978-1-951503-66-6 (Paperback)
ISBN: 978-1-951503-67-3 (ebook)

Authorsunite.com

If offense is herein proffered,
please take only what you need.

At a drug dealer's house somewhere in Canada a few years ago…

It was cold as fuck which somehow makes Canadian chicks even more badass - which is just crazy. Anyway…

Midway through the party this massive Canadian dude who looked like he preferred his maple syrup extra pulpy, and who was also an employee of our host, stands up, points at me, and begins to yell, "You know what? I think you're fucking full of shit, Motherfucker. Everything you've been saying since you've started talking is total bullshit. There is no fucking way any of that shit is true. You're a fucking liar."

My life's single greatest compliment.

David, Dani, and Ryker – THAT, my children… THAT is the goal:
A life of truth that defies belief.

I sucked at riding dirt until I realized that you don't ride ON a dirt bike. You run it like you do a chainsaw. You wield it. You throw it through the hairpins, you levitate above it through the washboards – it is You, not the bike that is soaring… you just use it however the fuck you can think of to get you there. Wield your life, my children. The seat is only there so you don't burn your ass on the battery.

It's a game. As if you've been given a whole, complete, and fully operational world all to yourself. Just for you. Well… you have. And your only obligation is to do whatever the fuck you want to do with it. Make every decision from your courage not your fear. You will always have that choice.

You are going to die. Get it? Good. Don't spend any more time on that one.

ALWAYS look cool. ALWAYS. If you don't feel cool, fucking STOP. You've lost your courage. Do not take another breath before you turn to find it.

Courage is life.

—Jason Lee Morrison

INTRODUCTION

One of my greatest fears has always been that everyone I know meet each other. Friends from my childhood as a missionary kid, Special Operations brothers from the military, bartenders, strippers, scientists, business friends and mentors from my professional life; and my beloved family. It's not because I am ashamed of any of them whatsoever. Quite the contrary. I deeply love and respect each and every one... I just know that they will all inadvertently offend the shit out of each other if ever they all should meet.

Friends change you because understanding them is part of it. You get to see shit from their perspective. I am the product of many perspectives. I can't blend in anymore. So, I'm not going to try. I'm going to abandon all pretense and just write true.

Ernest Hemingway used to say that he would be happy with just one "true" sentence. For me, a "true" sentence, and maybe for him too, will not only be true in the sense of a succinct and accurate representation of something, but it will also be the truth of me. The raw naked shit with no fat.

Furthermore, I'm going to write in the best possible way it can be written, but more importantly than that, even: in the best possible way it can be understood.

I think that is my responsibility before God and man and myself. So, I promise I'll do it.

The following is a chronological collection of my work since I made the conscious decision to be a writer. It will seem scattered and even contradictory as the passage of time attends to subject and style. The theme is the human condition. Most specifically, mine. What do war and art and the quest for truth have in common? In the maelstrom of a human life: Everything. It is a story. Not of the trials themselves, but of all the thought behind and in between the lines of them. This is my charred battleground. Where my ideas and questions and beliefs collide, much as my friends all would. I hope I have been courageous enough to step away and let them conflict. I hope it inspires you to be. This seldom traveled road is rife with fear and dead minds' bones. Reason is your compass. It points to even the incomprehensible truth.

WHAT WAR FEELS LIKE

My mouth is so dry. I can feel my heart beating, especially in my ears against the sweaty earpiece that I keep checking to make sure it's in tight, but the sweat won't let it be. I take a quick look around, then take my left glove off and roll a foamy piece of ear protection as tight as I can so it will fill up the ear canal and occlude as much sound as possible. The sweat and dirt on my fingers make it slippery as I roll it. I put it in my left ear and hold it there as it expands and makes the world sound dull and flat. Now I can't hear as well but once the shooting starts I won't hear anything at all if I don't put it in. It's a tradeoff. I put my glove back on then swear to myself and take it back off. I forgot I was going to put a dip in. The tobacco tastes cold and sweet between my gum and lip.

It's so hot you can smell it. Something is about to go down. Everyone can feel it. The shops started to close a few minutes ago, the proprietors pulling down the garage doors that open

1

to the dirty street. My back hurts from leaning back to counter the heavy ammo and grenades on the front of my ballistic plate carrier. I have 12 magazines on me and one in the gun totaling 390 rounds, and several types of grenades.

I'm aware that I am scared, and it pisses me off. I'm not scared of dying. I'm not scared of pain. I know beyond the shadow of a doubt that nothing will happen to me and I'm terrified of the shock and feeling of incredulity I will feel when it does. And I'm mad that I believe so strongly that nothing will kill me. It makes me feel like I'm not ready for something very big that I have to be ready for. It is insanely irritating. I feel daft. I keep trying to picture myself dead, or imagine the feeling of the explosion or bullet, so I'll be ready, but I can't. I'm not ready for death and it is infuriating.

I block it all out. But I'm still livid. I decide to take it for granted that I'm invincible. It's the best I can do.

The Marine Explosive Ordinance Disposal (EOD) guys are out on route Michigan getting ready to blow up a mortar round that failed to detonate upon impact of the street to my front. I'm in a reviewing stand about 10 feet off the ground and 10 feet from the road. 10 foot concrete Jersey barriers line the street in front of the Government Center compound where we are and continue around its border. Sandbags are stacked two wide and about 3 feet high around the circumference of the 20 X 10 foot reviewing stand floor. It has a tin roof and tin walls on three sides.

The Detail Leader, a former Delta Force guy named Pigpen, is sitting down in a folding metal chair with the PRC-119F radio handset jammed against his ear.

"They're going to blow it in 30 seconds." Pigpen says.

I take a hard look around before I get down behind the sandbags on a knee.

"CRACK"

The explosion is right next to us on the other side of the Jersey Barriers.

"Damn bro, that was a lot closer than I thought it was going to be." Pigpen laughs.

The explosion has a catalytic effect on the tension that has been mounting and now it breaks like a dam. We've all been waiting. Thank God, here we go.

Instantly rounds start snapping through the air by us. Sounds like maybe a PKM and some AK fire. The Marine Up-gunner's .50 cal is already answering.

Pigpen aims across my front and takes three shots.

I see nothing to my front and down the alleyway that I'm covering.

Suddenly it's dead quiet.

"Got that motherfucker." Pigpen says smiling. "He was in that one little window we were looking at yesterday."

I smile not taking my eyes off my sector of fire. I know it's going to kick off again in a second. I feel a lot better now.

IT

I tried to subdue it in the humid weight and rank of the Indonesian jungle.

It grew thick and heavy.

I tried to starve it in the high windswept cold of the Rockies.

It grew restless and wild.

I tried to wash it away in the harsh infinity of the Pacific.

It grew ominous and deep.

I tried to purge it in the strain and violence of the desert wars.

It grew bold and grave.

Then, unhinged, I turned to face it.

And it hurled itself at me like a monster.

It was not a demon as I had supposed.

It was a longing. A thirst.

It is this pen. This paper. This ink.

Right now is the most important time in your life.
It's the only time in your entire life that you can change it.

You can do nothing great until you can do something well.

EPIPHANY

Waiting for the epiphany.
Waiting.
Trying to ready yourself for it.
Like a fisherman fixated on the fly.
Anticipating the flash.
The strike.
The set of the hook.
The fight.
Hope.
The only thing left.
Hope.
Of one shot at a long shot.
To get what I want.
That's what I want.
No.
All I need is the epiphany.

Don't invest in the life that you have.
Invest in the life that you want.

I have learned to be wary of those who would
try to convince me to be less happy.

Somewhere out there I don't exist.
That's where I want to be.

It's we who helps us best.

When you dare to take that step.
When you leap into nothing.
And plummet from the heights.
If you are an eagle, then you will fly.
And if you are not. Then you won't.
But there is no other way to find out.
And there is no other way to learn how to fly.

THE HEAVY KIND
OF PAIN

It is a heavy kind of Pain.

That look of doubt
from a good friend.
To bear the ire
of the good men.

Kindly pitied
as if a fool
by those who once
believed in you.

And note the dis-
appointment from
Your last and great-
est champions.

To see those plead-
ing eyes that say:
"Oh, please don't throw
your life away.

Be strong and brave
to what is true.
Be what you'd want
your children to."

Conceding to
your errant way,
As long as you
return one day.

It is a heavy kind of Pain.

For when at last
I chased my dream,
They said I'd run
from everything.

I left the lie
for truth, in trade.
They said I'd thrown
my life away.

The bravest deed
in life I've done,
They say it was
a cowardly one.

For my children
I became a man.
They're told that I've
abandoned them.

When Nineveh
I finally found,
they said that I
was Joppa bound.

When I my great-
est calling win,
They'll say it is
my greatest sin.

It is a heavy kind of Pain.

I carry it
with no offense,
with love's sole
indifference.

For they are most,
dearest of friends,
And wish for me
the best of ends.

To do great things
they know I can
And be sought out
from other men.

Just as those who know
the gods' true voice
seek men to build
their dreams of choice.

They seek only
the best of men.
And I will not
be one of them.

For theirs I'll not
put mine a-shelf,
For I can hear
the gods myself.

As long as you are OK nothing will change for you.
Wake up and dream.
You have settled for the possible.
But you cannot do the impossible.
You can only become it.

TO A FRIEND ON MEMORIAL DAY

Thanks for being one of the few who has truly risked it all. You know the price. I've watched miracles unfold before my eyes more than once that spared my life and don't understand how or why, when so many better than me were not similarly spared. All I can do is thank those who were willing, though not called upon to pay with their lives, and remember the fallen. This requires for us, their comrades, no effort or compulsion because their faces and characters are forever branded upon our souls. So, I'll do for them only what I'd ask be done for me today: feel no guilt. Feel no pity. Remember their strength. And carry on the way we fought together: with sheer sacrificial love and ferocity, making every minute count on their behalf as well as ours as if we carried them along with us every day. Because we do.

It's the best of us all who fights best for
what's best for the rest of us all.

Each sensation that caused us pain made us laugh the more.

You who trust many know but a few pains.
You who trust none know but a few friends.

Peace has never been achieved by inaction.
War has never been achieved without it.

PTSD

At first, I thought it was my appetites.
They seemed ravenous and unsatiated.
Then I noticed it.
The absence of the taste of sensation.
Every indulgence was in the hope of it.
But there was none.
Life tastes like white chalk.
It all tastes exactly the same to me.
The worst part is that I can remember what it was like to taste.
Both the good and the bad.
The good I still pursue, but in too great a quantity.
The bad... the unthinkable, I do in search of any taste at all.
Yet, the only lingering taste is that of shame.
And that makes it even worse.
Because I don't taste it nearly as much as I ought to.

22 Pushups a day will never stop the bleeding of the 22 veterans we're losing every day to suicide and will definitely give no hope or resource to those living in the drab grey world of PTSD. I've called the hotline before, myself. Unless we can show each other how to think our way through this shit, nothing will ever change. No doctor or counselor who has never experienced it will ever be able to do this for us. We must do it for ourselves and shine the light back on the trail for those behind us.

THE WAY YOU ARE

Pick whichever God you would prefer to beat you.
All of us are dogs owned by animals that eat you.
Come believe in me, I won't hesitate to beat you.
I will be your God and you will let me defeat you.
You will praise my name because I did not delete you.
Even though the battle's lost, I will not retreat you.
But you may die for me, and I will consecrate you.
And kill for me so that I may fully dominate you.
Give all to me unselfishly and I will tolerate you.
Slander my conspiracy and I will intimidate you.
Go and sin and fail again so I may liberate you.
And owe to me eternally, otherwise I'll hate you.
And cast your damn-ed soul to hell and fully violate you.
Until the end when I descend to obliterate you.
So, get on your knee and worship me and I'll claim to create you.
Now feel the shame to think again. See how I manipulate you?

You don't see things the way they are.
You see things the way you are.

THE CALL-OUT

Bloody and beleaguered,
man stands, unsteady atop
the rubble of this earth,
and cries to the Gods:
"We get along?
NO! You get along!
Fuck you!"

If all roads lead to God, why is the middle man-
agement telling us to kill each other?

There's been some confusion on the meaning of this piece. It's
harsh. But it should be. You ought to be offended. Choose not
to take offense at its vulgarity, that is to tempt you away from
being enraged at its veracity.

If the Masters of all the religions in the world are real, if all
paths lead to God, then why are we destroying each other over
their inability to reconcile? Tolerance. What a sick delusion.

Would you tolerate your sick child being prescribed the wrong medicine? The existence of many powerful lies does not prove the nonexistence of truth. It does matter what you believe. The defiance of man against lies is merited. Hatred toward the deceived is abhorrent. Tolerance of enslavement to lies is disgusting. The truth alone will reconcile us to each other. Liars be damned. Gods or no.

Prayers are the little clouds that form beneath your feet
when you are walking on nothing at all.

The Bible is thought to not stand against science and reason.
Do not expect this generation to believe
in anything not reasonable,
whether or not the reason is known.

THE FOOL

I thought the first one would be easiest. It wasn't. Not even close. The easiest step was an accident. And years since the first. And it was wrought by the only thing more dense and impenetrable and ominous than jungle: the dirt and rock and ice that erupted immediate and vertical and eternal and immense and motionless as nothing and daunting as fuck before me: the mountain.

I stumbled back a step when I saw it. That was the easiest one. And the lightest. Jungle had torn all from me but rags. It's been as long now since the easiest step as the easiest was from the first. But others have joined me here. And have since been taught to be, each by the other, masters of our severe environs. Enough even to create and craft and tool and replenish all that we agreed we could not live without, and more in fact.

We can find no way up it, no matter how many implements we can all together carry. And only who've surmounted jungle have mettle enough for the burden. Close as brothers and well equipped, our camp is strong now here. We've only ever lost but one. It still pains me.

He stayed for but a night. Seemed almost put off by our welcome invitation and our grave initiation the evening he came in. And by the morning light was gone as ghost. We found but all left of his kit and rags at the base of the cruel mountain scarred by a scrawl in the dirt: "All that can keep you from all you want most, is all you want less."

Seems the poor damn fool tried to climb it. He betrayed us all. Poor stupid wretched fuck.

17 JUNE 2016
ENTEBBE, UGANDA

This is in response to a question in Visitor Posts.

Post: Hello Sir, I randomly came across u and your writing via Howzit Jinja. So, I guess you accomplished your goal by posting on there. I have read 3-4 of your timeline posts. I find your perspective and writing thoughtful and to some extent fascinating. Mostly, I am fascinated by the fact that you write and post these thoughts in a public way. I have 2 questions for you: 1) how do you make money in UG? It almost feels to me, you've written some of these things out of necessity, forceful passion. 2) what is the underlying reasoning for posting these things? I find it hard to believe that you just want to stir the pot. Do you feel you are contributing to the world via your posts and writing? If so, in what way? Feel free to not respond at all; as well, feel free to respond via PM

Response: Thanks for tracking me down through the Howzit Jinja page and taking the time to look over my stuff. Mostly, thank-you for the questions. They are direct, some are difficult, and all of them seem to have a reason for being asked. Those are good questions, and I will answer them all with the truth they merit.

Firstly, I did accomplish my goal! But my goal was not to peddle my writing. I have met you, and I hope it will lead to meeting you and other Jinja-ites in person.

Some background: I was born in the US, but when I was 2 my parents moved to Indonesia. I grew up there until I graduated high school. We got there in 1979. My dad used to fly around over the jungle, hours by air away from any kind of civilization. He and his fellow missionaries would look for smoke coming up from the jungle below. If and when they spotted smoke, they would mark it on a map, then spend weeks hiking through Sulawesi's mountains and triple canopy rain forests to see if they could make contact with the people groups who's smoke they had spotted from the air. These people were as primitive as you can get. They had only occasionally met anyone from the coast to trade rattan and rubber for leaf springs to make machetes and spear heads, wire and bicycle inner tubes for their spear guns, salt, and other necessities of war and life. Their whole world since the beginning of the earth had been only them and the jungle with the few other equally primitive tribes who they were constantly at war with. They called themselves the people of Bahasa Madi: The people of the language of "NO". They were all about 5 feet tall or less, each tribe's trappings were unique, but all wore only a loin cloth, a small pouch for their betel nut, a razor-sharp machete, it's handle adorned with human hair from the heads they had taken, each in an ornately carved scabbard tied with wicker weaved rope around their waist. Leather would rot in the jungle. Two bamboo tubes about a foot long tied together and filled with blow- gun darts. The poison for the darts was there, ready, in the recess of the bamboo lid in the form of a dark tar-like substance. The blowguns were 8 feet long and their spears 12 or more. Some carried short daggers with L-shaped handles and blades treated with poison, the blades intentionally rusted so that the poison was within the powdery rust. They lived in houses which were at least 20-30 feet off the ground to keep enemies within their own or other tribes from spearing them through the floor while they slept. Constant wars and vendettas. They did have medicine. From the Dūkung. The witchdoctor who communed with the demons and ancestors that dominated their daily lives through taboos, curses, and the like. In one tribe, for instance, it was taboo to cut the grains of rice from the stalk unless done from directly behind it. A trespass would be found out and punished severely, sometimes by death, lest the tribe bear the ever-present wrath of the spirits they worshiped. The spirits of the trees and mountains and rocks. I saw a look in their eyes I will never forget.

When I returned to the US at the age of 18, I joined the US Marine Corps. I was in a Special Operations unit called Force Recon. It's what people would call Special Forces. Altogether, I worked in units like this for 16 years, all over the world. In wars you've probably forgotten, or maybe didn't even know about. I've never been to France or Switzerland or Monaco, but I've been all over this planet. They don't send you to places like that. They send you where there is pain. But I have been to some wonderful places too. I was a businessman in Washington DC for several years and have traveled all over the world, from one Business Class lounge to the next. Four Star Hotels weren't good enough for me, neither was a Toyota, or a Casio, or an ink pen that costed less than $200. Yes, I bought into it, hook line and sinker. A friend of mine spent $15,000.00 USD for two nights at a hotel in Dubai, just because, at the time it was the most expensive hotel in the world. I haven't been a millionaire, but I've come pretty damned close. Then I lost it all. Everything. In one day. I'm glad I don't have that life anymore. I don't like who I was. Don't get me wrong. I'm not apologizing for anything. Making money is one of the hardest things to do in the whole world. Everyone is trying to do it. If you're good at it, and fair, my hat is off to you, and I hope you enjoy spending it. I might still get rich one day.

I've invented a few things that might be novel. But not right now. This is too important. I need to write. That's why I came here. One-way ticket. Just to write. No job. No money. Just an invitation from my best friend to stay with him and his wife in Entebbe. And write. It was a giant leap of faith. The bravest thing I've ever done. Everyone, even long-time friends and mentors told me it was a bad idea. And it's been the most amazing time of my entire life. Read "The Heavy Kind of Pain", and you'll get the play-by-play. Since then I've found a job supervising the construction of a University Campus here in Uganda.

But I won't stop writing. I can't. To answer your question, I don't get paid for any of my work. As of now I have not even tried to. I'd love to be able to make a living with just my writing, and I'd like to get there, but I don't even know what that would look like. Poetry hasn't been cool since Edgar Allan Poe. I don't think that will change too much. You're right about one thing specifically, and I'm very glad that you caught it. These are ideas. They may or may not rhyme, but they are not just cute little words that sound pretty together. I sure hope not anyway. The purpose of Art ought to be to facilitate the creation of new ideas in the mind of the reader. To see things differently, or to think about something in a way that you've never thought of it before. So, if you want to get people to get honest with themselves, that's the best way to reach them, but honestly, I'm a writer. That's it. It's all I've got. So that's what I use. So, what's it all about? I guess it would look like I'm just trying to get attention, or stir the pot, as you say. I'm glad that you asked that because my motives for writing this stuff surely come into question by a reader, and I don't want that to distract them from the important stuff.

You know that look I mentioned in the eyes of those tribal people on the island of Sulawesi. Do you know why I'll never forget it? Or why I felt compelled to foist my life story upon you? It's because I've seen people in every stage of cultural evolution. From the tribal person in a loin cloth, to the businessman in a $10,000 suit. And everything in between. And in every context from war to opulent luxury verging on the ridiculous. We all have one thing in common. Some have more diversions than others, so it's harder to see, but it's there. It's right out in front for the people of Bahasa Madi, or that little girl gazing out into nothing, standing by the road in the war-ravaged bedlam that was once the town of Ar Ramadi, Iraq. There are no diversions for them. They face it every second. They have to. They are afraid. They are uncertain. Of everything. They don't understand. And they have lost hope in ever finding an answer. It's in their eyes. And the reason I'll never forget it is that I see it every single day. That same look is in the eyes of all of us. Of every human being who, at the very core of who they are, when all the rest is stripped away, are certain beyond any doubt of only one thing: They don't know the truth.

It doesn't matter if the truth exists, or if it doesn't. If it's possible to find, or not. They don't know it. All that they know is that the fear is still there. The uncertainty. And the hopeless bewilderment. In its purest form it is expressed in the face of a newborn child who feels the sharp sensation of pain. With every possible facility of expression its bewildered soul cries out only one enormous question: "WHY?"

And we have no answer to give it. Because we have none for ourselves. And this is the human condition. And it breaks my fucking heart. Because I know what the truth is.

I have no fear. I know my destiny. And I don't like the answer, but I know "Why". My life is far more than the breaths that I take. Live is a verb. And it has been given to me as such. I am a free man. So, when I see that look in people's eyes. And I know that I know what can set them free. What enrages me more than anything on this earth, is the power of lies against truth. That even if I lay the truth out before them, the lies they believe will reject it. Or embrace but mutate it into another lie. For if truth is "adjusted" one iota, it is no longer truth. It can't be. If it is not exclusive of everything but itself, it is not. There is only one truth. And its greatest enemies are the lies that it does not exist, that it is all incomprehensible, and its own distortion. The less distorted, the more insidious is the lie that it becomes, because it looks so much like the truth. It is counterfeit. No matter how good the quality, it is still counterfeit.

So, I'm not trying to "Stir the pot", if you mean that I just want to be controversial. I don't give a shit about creating controversy. In fact, it becomes a huge distraction from my aim. Assumptions are another huge distractor. Assumptions of my aim, or of my message. You see, in many cases, there is no message. I just want to make you think. I'm not going to foist my beliefs on anyone else. Why should they believe me? Why not some other self-proclaimed prophet? My aim is to help them identify the lies that they believe in. We all believe in lies and don't know it. Whether it's about who we are, or our self-worth, our abilities, potential, or even about the nature of money. We all lean on false beliefs. Only when we remove them do we see actual change in ourselves and our behavior. You'll never be skinny enough, if you believe you look fat. Only when you see the lie and remove it, can you see yourself as you really are. In truth. See what I mean? The truth is there. We just don't see it because there is a lie in the way. That's why I don't feel that I have to tell you what to believe...not that it would work anyway. If I help show people how to spot lies, the truth will emerge. And it may even surprise you what the truth is. You may have looked right at it before and missed it. Because you weren't ready to receive it. There was a lie in its place.

And I want people to know how to recognize the lies that surround the truth. So, if they choose to, they can reject what they know in their hearts to be bullshit because it doesn't make any sense. Truth is reasonable. It is logical. Many lies will tell you not to use reason, especially when it comes to things like God. They will say that you must rely solely on faith. That's a sneaky one because it's almost true. You definitely must rely on faith to be able to accept a being capable of willing this universe into existence. That kind of being is incomprehensible to us just as infinity is. But just as infinity is incomprehensible, it is not untrue. Reason shows us that infinity is true even though we cannot comprehend it. In the same way, we must rely on faith

IN THE TRUTH to arrive at a true but incomprehensible being. Belief systems that throw out reason subvert any possibility to validate their claims of truth. Very sly. But the lie is easily spotted. If they proclaim a supreme being and source of existence, surely its attributes are represented within that which the being has brought into existence. And they are. The universe functions on order, logic, and reason. So, to say then that you must abandon reason in order to understand the source of existence of a logical universe is stupid. It makes no sense. It is a lie. Reject it. If such a being exists, it will by nature be fantastic and inexplicable. If it is not, it is surely a concept from the mind of a man. And if it is not, why believe in it? I cannot even comprehend my own mind, so if I can comprehend such a being, it is less than me. I will just believe in myself and be done with it. Religion does this. It makes God small enough for us to understand, but not big enough to be God. So, people choose to believe in their religion instead of their God, because their God is impotent. Even those closest to the truth do this. Many of them know the truth, but they don't believe that it is true. They don't know well enough to be sure. They are just as afraid as everyone else. So, they have made the truth into a religion. Then believe and place their trust in their religion, not in their God.

So, the reason I write what I do is that I want to give people the courage and understanding to defy the lies. To seek the truth. And don't dare settle for anything less. If you seek the truth with all your heart, you will find it. This is True. And the Truth will set you free.

Had Shakespeare written as his heroes did
we'd none of us know his name.

You can become who everyone says you ought to be,
or you can become who you have always been.
But you cannot be both.
And when you find yourself becoming yourself,
you will turn to find others following you.
They are trying to become who everyone says they ought to be.

Dream big.
You would if your dreams were glimpses of your future.
Well... they are.

For Alex. Happy Birthday.
Kampala, Uganda

Tears mean that you're learning something important.

Happiness is not found in fun.
It's found in peace.

I was taught this, then I learned it, then I stole it.
Now I'm giving it back...for Pier

We all need a battle.

We tear away at time who most revile what's passed.

Here's a little secret for the rest of you:
With us, battle is not an obligation to a friend.
It is an invitation from a brother.

We forge each our own sword with our life's mettle.
And we carry it with us throughout eternity.

It's not all about money.
But alot of it is all about money.

You can know everything and still be wrong.
It's not about just what you know.
It's about how you think about what you know.

You see, there are no "deals" to make with God. If you believe that I made you to be the most amazing thing I've ever done, if you believe that I think you are beautiful beyond description, because I'm a master artist, and Dude, I'm God, so I'm pretty much the best there is. And I made you so fucking well, that I am even amazed by you. Why do you think everyone outside of your few dimensions is enamored with you in some good or evil way?

You are exquisite on the level of the Almighty GOD.

If you believe that, you will see and live your life in a new and different way. You will become more like me.

And I AM Love.

Trust me on this one.

—Jesus

SO BE IT

I will pass it all by.
I do not even know if my destination exists.
But I know the direction it lies.
I will swim past the rest.
If it exists or not, I do not know,
but that's where I'm going.
You may lose sight of me for awhile.
Or for forever.
I do not know.
But if you see me again, I will be the king of this life.
I will not settle for anything you can imagine.
I will not settle for it until it has surpassed possibility.
God damn it.
If it's achievable, I will surpass it.
That's where I'm headed.
And if I should drown or be found lacking,
so be it.

WELL, THAT SHIT'S OVER

I guess I figured it out somehow…finally.
Somewhere along the way I started to believe that no one wanted me.
So, I started giving myself away.
For cheap.
Expecting nothing.
And getting it.
But they didn't want me.
I was right about that.
They maybe wanted the idea of me.
Anyway. This hurts. Writing it all down.
Explains a lot. I can't write the rest.
Not like this, anyway.
Well… that shit's over.

Thanks, J.
Love you, man.

TURNING POINT

There's a drunk girl swaying at my once peaceful table.
And a guy begging for a beating, but I'm just not able.
I'm at peace with it all.
Like never before.
It's almost last call.
It's a quarter to four.
"Piano Man" is playing.
And the world is just right.
For the first time I remember,
In all of my life.

LANA DEL REY

I hear the lines
that bear your rhymes,
defiant to the last.....
They without fail,
taste rail by rail
as off a stripper's ass.

Easily one of the best writers alive today.

God ain't stupid. He knows there's
going to be some frustration.

I went through it all.
After awhile I didn't really know what it was to be afraid.
I've faced the worst of it.
You don't know.
I want to protect you from ever having to learn it.
I guess that's paternalistic.
But you are so happy in your ignorance,
I want you to keep it if you can.

I have to admit it.
Deep down I wanted the pain.
Somehow, I knew it was my only way out of hell.

Everywhere I look they tell me who to hate
And should I not consent
I suffer the same fate.

DREAD

I was a better man back then.

Striving in the bosom of fear.

It was always there.

Like a soul craving spectre.

It's my own demon.

I've carried it since I can remember.

I secretly despised those without the curse.

Pathetic breathers of tortured men's air.

Who did not deserve an ounce of pain.

Crushed by it since my memory began:

dread of the ordinary life.

BLACK

To my black fellow Americans:
You are up against it. Hard.
That's for sure.
I think we all see that something needs to change.
First, I think you need to recognize who you are.
What you have done in this world.
You are a new culture, you see.
You were torn out of your old one long ago.
What you have made in your new one is all yours.
It does not come from Africa.
It comes from you.
You are young.
Not even as old as our flag.
And in that time, you have changed the world.
There is no culture in all this world that you have not somehow affected.
Be proud of the heritage that you are creating.
The healing must come from within.

You must do it.
You must do it for yourselves.
We stand by you.
But this must come from you.
Not born of inequality but born of self-respect.
Of ownership.

Black minds matter.
The world needs you.

DELIGHT

"Show me your beauty," I said to you, Lord.
You showed me my vanity.
I said, "take it away."
You said, "where is your delight?"
I said, "I delight myself in you."
You said, "Beneath your vanity is your delight, just as you left it
when you were a child...
and seeing you thus is my delight. For it is you - my reflection
- my image - you who
reflect me... you humans all. Your delight is my beauty."

PURE

I didn't know that pain had so many flavors.
Or that everything I can feel can hurt so bad.
All at once.
For so long.
Like waiting till you're told you can breathe.
When the pain squeezes so hard that it all just crushes out of you.
Like the apple press.
Dripping the bile and blood of my soul.
Pulp and peel are gone.
Refuse.
Waste.
I am all that is left of me.
I am pure.

THAT'S PEACE

I've been in the desert before.
Walking.
Through the sand.
Hours.
No water.
120 lbs of equipment and a rifle.
The God damn sun.
All you could think about was water.
It would defy any king's ransom to you.
The horizon is so far away.
And I don't yet see our destination upon it.

And then it's finally over.
And you can see the water.
And know that it's real.
And know that you're about to taste it.
Then it rolls out like sex across the tongue.

And you swallow its filling wetness like the taste of life itself.
And you're whole.
And quenched.
Stupefied.
It's over.

that's peace

Parts of the game are shit.
But the game itself is a beautiful one.

I used to think that if I lived past 30
I wasn't trying hard enough.
I still don't know if that's true, or not.
I might have had the number wrong.

Happiness is a decision.
Not a destination.

And gratitude is its "EASY" button.

There are but few who deserve to die at war.
The rest of us die in our beds.

We are each given one chance to rule the world.

We all think we're failing because we can't stop sinning,
and some of us are tired of giving a fuck.

... until we begin to understand:
it's the sin that's killing us,
not the sentence.
It's its own judgement.

A problem is just the asshole of an opportunity.
If you're always covered in shit, you might
be focused on the wrong things.

THAT, MY DEAR, IS LOVE

If you can love your naked self so much to take the risk of embracing that of me which is most vulnerable, inside the safety of your deepest self, where you are most delicate... and if you let me explore you, and find where we feel each the other most, you will find a mystery: that somehow the sensation of my firmness, and strength, wrapped inside you, against the most tender delicate parts of you, is softer than the memory of silk.

It is more than touch. It is pure consummation of trust that all of each of us that can touch the other, no matter how strong, or harsh, or rough, will only ever conjoin in this mysterious kiss, where our greatest, and deepest, and most tender vulnerabilities embrace.

That, My Dear, is love.

A WOMAN WHO OWNS IT

There is nothing sexier on a woman than ambition, and nothing more elegant than authenticity. Elegance is but supreme fearlessness wrapped in silk.

Women have a power that no man can touch. Fear is its great nemesis. Vanity makes it look cheap. When you see a woman like Audrey Hepburn, it's there. A woman whose courage and grace overcome her fear and vanity to expose the fierce and immutable power of a woman. It's mesmerizing.

I'm an adventurer. I'm a man. I'm a bit reckless and I'm not afraid of anything. I place a high premium on propriety and class, a lack thereof is juvenile. I smoke, I drink, and I cuss… a lot. I like Texas hold'em over Blackjack because I like long odds. I take risks. I'm compassionate. It takes courage. Tolerance requires nothing of you. It's a waste. I was a fat kid so I despise meanness. I have a premonition that I will be wildly successful in some way. It won't change anything. I love like I live. (It sounds cliché' but it's true.): stuck on full throttle with no brakes. It's just the way it is, so I've had to learn to turn quick and crisp.

That's the truth about me.

I was close, but I was wrong... it's not Audrey Hepburn, it's Adria Dunn.

Here's to you Adria.

Quit trying to be a better person.
You'd be a great person right now if you
could just hold your shit together.
Focus on that instead.

Never concede that you are lesser than you are
that you may gain the approval
of those who have given up on challenging themselves.
You may be their only hope.

CHI

If you, the latest, brightest apple of my eye,
would condescend to meet again, though I have wrought your ire,
I would that you would bring a friend,
of Bourbon, or of Rye... but please come...

You see that all that you don't know of me,
could fill the basin of the sea,
and still spread intrigue on the shore,
like beer froth spilling o'er the bar.

You've never met a man like me,
nor any man that I can see,
they're all afraid of living still,
but none have seen the torture mill.
Or they who have keep to themselves,
and laugh at all the world calls pain,
cause we've been there and back again.

And coming back… Is so god damn beautiful.

It's like watching a flower blossom.
From the inside.

And live.
And God Damn live.

So…
If you're fucking up my chi, I'm out.

Tired of everyone else constantly thinking badly about you?
Don't worry. They're not.
You are thinking about you.
They are thinking about them.
Feel better?

IT'S ALL JUST AS LIKELY A PLOP OF GOD SHIT.

THE ANNIHILATION OF NOTHING AND THE ADVENT OF EXISTENCE

Everything is made of something.

Nothing is made of nothing.

And do not be so foolish as to equate "0" to nothing.

"0" is something. And its presence brings with it tenants of reason, which is something.

Nothing is not a vacuum. It is not empty space. It is not even infinity. It is No Thing and therefore bears no meaning. And it is all pervasive. For if something were to exist, it would infinitely replace nothing. Our so called "laws of the universe" point to it, just as they point to the concept of infinity, which is also incomprehensible, in spite of our awareness of it.

Aristotle's definition of nothing is the closest one can come to its comprehension: "Nothing is what rocks dream about."

Curiously, there cannot exist one elemental thing. One thing is not enough to exist. For, one thing existent alone is singularly pervasive and equally as meaningless as nothing. And the absence of meaning is nothing, for something has meaning, nothing does not, not only that, but there is no object to which its meaning (if it had any) to be meaningful to. There is no "quantum observer". If it is not _____, then it is not. It cannot be a question mark. Again, "Nothing" is pervasive. Everything is nothing, or nothing is nothing. The advent of "something" then, means that the "something" is everything. If there is but one thing, and it is not, then it is all of nothing, and "nothing" is everything.

Two things cannot exist.

Only three can. The introduction of a second thing brings with it a third, for two things relate. Relationship is as elemental as the elements it relates and does not exist between fewer than two of them.

$$\underline{0 \pm 1} = 3$$

Therefore, there is nothing if there is not three things. And the advent of existence is the advent of meaning, for meaning is not existent apart from at least two different elements in relationship which can then bear and emit meaning through the relationship of more than one pervasive thing and meaning is then born through relationship of two different elements which have meaning one to the other. For if the two elements were the same, there would be no meaning one to the other, therefore no relationship would exist between them for they are the same and then only one thing, which, again, is nothing.

If you now say there are more than three elements, you have surpassed the fundaments of existence. Therefore, the basis of everything existent is only exactly the three elements with which existence is comprised. To say that there is a fourth element is to say that it exists, and nothing can exist if not existent of three elements, and if that already exists, existence is "accomplished" and infinitely pervasive, leaving no room for anything other than its triune singularity.

For none of the three elements exist alone. They cannot. They are existent only in this trinity. This trinity alone exists. It is everything that is and all that there is. Its presence eternally displaces "Nothing" which, by its own definition, never was.

$$\underline{3} = 1$$

Because it is all that is, and pervasively existent, and there can be no room in existence for any other thing, the question arises as to the nature of the "visceral" existence of our universe. It seems reasonable to believe that it may be comprised of a seemingly intentional and intelligent projection/emission of this trinity. The "universe" would not then be infinite, per se, but infinitely comprised of infinity through projection/emission thereof.

This non-lineal, third party projection concept gives room to the inclusion of otherwise incompatible rules such as the conundrum of Quantum Theory vs. Einstein's Theory of Relativity. These rules do not have to be relative to each other, only bonded, and there are likely others, yet undiscovered, beyond the range of our current capacity to observe.

IMPLICATIONS OF THE PROJECTION CONCEPT

This concept serves to raise more acute reason regarding the nature of our context of thought toward our visceral existence and environment. Science is but discovery, measurement, and attribution of meaning, (tools such as mathematics are but derivatives thereof). It is a product of the human drive to project meaning upon its environment. (A seeming and curious shared attribute with this trinity.) To ascribe meaning, we must have knowledge. To gain knowledge, we must measure. To measure, we must have "size". Size is a human construct bounded by linear human thought process, but it works fairly well. It is helpful but not reasonable. In order to establish a baseline from which size can be derived, we must have a universal constant. But there is no edge against which to calibrate our measurement…so we made ourselves the baseline, (the ancient unit of measure called the Cubit, for example, is the distance between a human's elbow to fingertips, approximately 18 inches.) Everything is either bigger or smaller than us. In front of or behind. Closer or further. Faster or slower. We created measure to inform quantity, which we created, then we began to see the entirety of existence through this self-created lens. Then we taught ourselves to regard human perspective as an infallible universal baseline. Then we taught ourselves to regard anything beyond our ability to quantify by rules of our own rudimentary contrivance as absurd.

Our visceral existence does however seem reasonable because most of it that we can measure complies, of course, with the fixed nature of our systems of measure. It might well be that we will never understand those things of our existence which do not cooperate with the rules within which our systems of measure are bounded. For if visceral existence is infinitely comprised of infinity, no constant exists nor can. The statement itself: "uniform infinity" is absurd.

THERE'S A BIG BANG IN THE BIBLE, BOYS AND GIRLS

Imagine that you are a scientist with the task of explaining the concepts of Space, Matter, Energy, and Time to primitive people of the earth from several thousand years ago. They have no written language, and no words for these concepts in their spoken language. What, from their environment, would you use to communicate these concepts to them? Go ahead. Answer the question in your own mind, then keep reading...

These seem to be the most reasonable metaphors for their context and understanding:
Space: the sky, the night sky especially. We'll call it "the heavens"
Matter: dirt or earth, water. We'll call it "earth" or "water".
Energy: the warming light of the sun. We'll use "light".

Time: The track of the celestial bodies across the sky/motion.

These things, of course, exist in their own right, so when you are referring to the actual things themselves, such as the heavens, the earth, light, and time, and not the metaphors, you would have to define them as themselves when the actual things come into your narrative, and thereafter, depart from the metaphorical use of them. For example, if I tell you that I'll be using the word "heavens" to mean "space", I would then be compelled to tell you when I depart from the metaphor and again begin using "heavens" only to mean "heavens".

So, with that being said, let's look at Genesis 1, the first book of the Bible. We'll use the standard convention of Verses in the Bible (e.g. *V1*) as references.

V1. In the beginning God created the heavens [space] *and the earth* [matter].

This makes sense scientifically, because matter cannot exist without the space that it occupies, therefore space would come before matter.

V2. The earth [matter] *was formless and void, and darkness was over the surface of the deep, and the Spirit of God was moving over the surface of the waters* [matter].

The Hebrew word for "the deep" is תְהוֹם "tehom" or תְהֹם "tehom", which also means "abyss". It can also mean "sea", but "sea" is not defined as such until verse 10, later in the story, when it says: *God called the dry land earth, and the gathering of the waters He called seas.* So, we will continue with "earth" and "water" as metaphors for matter until we get there. So, as matter is, of course, not just a solid, but also liquid, gas, etc, "the deep", or "abyss" could indicate some kind of primordial soup. This makes a lot of sense when we see that the matter was "*formless* (Hebrew: הַ

ו "tohu" – chaos, confusion, meaningless) *and void* (Hebrew: וּהֹב "bohu" – emptiness)". Therefore, it appears as though "the earth", "the deep", and "the waters" in this verse are all referring to the same thing. They are all being used metaphorically in an attempt to describe this primordial soup.

V3. Then God said, "Let there be light"; and there was light.

In verse 14 it says: *Then God said, "Let there be lights..."* This is when the celestial bodies that give us light are defined, therefore, until we get there, we will consider the light in verse 3 to be our metaphor for energy because in verse 3 above, as no source of light is defined, and according to the laws of the Universe that God is creating, light emanates from a source, it doesn't make any sense unless it is being used as a metaphor for something else. I've heard people say that the light came from God Himself, but as God is everywhere, there would be no way for Him to separate light from darkness, as that would directly contradict the scripturally validated claim to God's omnipresence. So, now we have Space, Matter, and Energy, and we are still within the bounds of the Physical Laws of the burgeoning Universe.

V4. God saw that the light was good; and God separated the light from the darkness.

Energy, by its very nature, possesses a positive or negative force. This could speak to this delineation but it could also speak to the "formless and void" statement in verse 2: *formless* (Hebrew: תהֹו "tohu" – chaos, confusion, meaningless) *and void* (Hebrew: וּהֹב "bohu" – emptiness)". This light could mean more or different than simply "energy". This could represent the introduction of the dichotomy of meaning and chaos. It could well represent the "laws" within which the universe will function.

V5. God called the light day, and the darkness He called night. And there was evening and there was morning, one day.

The 24 hour day is not defined, or even definable until verse 14: *Then God said, "Let there be lights in the expanse of the heavens to separate the day from the night..."* There can be no measurement of time without motion. Evening and morning indicate the advent of Motion although there is as yet no way to measure it until verse 14. Evening and morning are also indicators of time that the people of that age would be familiar with, and so it is used here as a metaphor, for their sake. Furthermore, while word used here for *day* (Hebrew: יוֹם, yom) is commonly used to refer to a 24 hr period of time, it is also used in other places to mean "age" or "epoch". Daniel 12:13 *But as for you, go your way to the end; then you will enter into rest and rise again for your allotted portion at the end of the <u>age</u>.* The use of the words *And there was evening and there was morning, one day,* is also unique to this part of the scriptures and as it is first used here, could hint at an alternative meaning to its most common use as a 24 hr day, which the Hebrews define as from evening to evening, not evening to morning. Notice that from evening to morning is from dark to light, from chaos to order. It could also mean the end of an epoch and the beginning of a new one which is most likely why in Gen 2:1-3 where it talks about the 7th and final day, when God rests, it does not say "and there was evening and there was morning a 7th day." It is likely that we are still in the "7th day". This passage in Hebrews 4:3-7 could well point to this:

3 For we who have believed enter that rest, just as He has said,
"AS I swore in MY wrath,
They shall not enter MY rest,"
although His works were finished from the foundation of the world.
4 For He has said somewhere concerning the seventh day: "And God rested on the seventh day from all His works"; 5 and again in this passage, "They shall not enter MY rest." 6 Therefore, since it remains for some to enter it, and those who formerly had good news preached to them failed to enter because of disobedience, 7 He again fixes a certain day, "Today," saying through David after so long a time just as has been said before,

*"Today if you hear His voice,
DO not harden your hearts."*

The *"rest"* mentioned throughout these verses, and all throughout the book of Hebrews, in fact, could well be the same rest as the 7th day rest. It certainly seems so here: *4 For He has said somewhere concerning the seventh day: "And God rested on the seventh day from all His works"; 5 and again in this passage, "They shall not enter MY rest."* Therefore, it would appear that *"Today"* in Hebrews 4:7 is the 7th day. We are still in the 7th day, or 7th epoch.

V6. Then God said, "Let there be an expanse in the midst of the waters, and let it separate the waters from the waters."

BANG! In the book Industrial Explosion Prevention and Protection, Frank T. Bodurtha defines an explosion as such: "an explosion is the result, not the cause, of a rapid expansion of gases. It may occur from physical or mechanical change." Basically, God blows the primordial soup apart with an explosion.

V7. God made the expanse, and separated the waters which were below the expanse from the waters which were above the expanse; and it was so.

The words "below" and "above" are actually the same Hebrew word: מִן "min" or יִנִּי "minni" or יַנֵּמ "mine". This basically means that the matter was separated apart, one from the other, within the expanse of space, or *expanse of the heavens* as outer space is defined in the next verse and in verse 15: *for lights in the expanse of the heavens to give light on the earth...*

V8. God called the expanse heaven. And there was evening and there was morning, a second day.

Not until verse 8 is the word "heaven" ascribed to its actual meaning of the sky and outer space, but hereafter it carries that meaning because it has been defined as such. It is no longer used as a metaphor for Space. The second and ensuing days denote the continuation of consistent motion according to the same Physical Laws that governed the first day.

V9. Then God said, "Let the waters below the heavens be gathered into one place, and let the dry land appear"; and it was so.

After the explosion, the universe begins to form from the elemental level and below. Gravity begins to gather matter into what are now the celestial bodies. Order is introduced to what was chaos: "formless and void" v2. Specifically, on earth, this is happening, but it is also happening generally throughout the Universe.

V10. God called the dry land earth, and the gathering of the waters He called seas; and God saw that it was good.

Again, earth and water are here defined and depart forever from their metaphorical meanings. While this is going on throughout the universe on other planets and celestial bodies, this is the definitive transition from speaking of the Universe to now speaking of the planet Earth. Why? Because this record is for the people of earth.

V11. Then God said, "Let the earth sprout vegetation, plants yielding seed, and fruit trees on the earth bearing fruit after their kind with seed in them"; and it was so.

V12. The earth brought forth vegetation, plants yielding seed after their kind, and trees bearing fruit with seed in them, after their kind; and God saw that it was good.

V13. There was evening and there was morning, a third day.

V14. Then God said, "Let there be lights in the expanse of the heavens to separate the day from the night, and let them be for signs and for seasons and for days and years;

V15. and let them be for lights in the expanse of the heavens to give light on the earth"; and it was so.

V16. God made the two great lights, the greater light to govern the day, and the lesser light to govern the night; He made the stars also.

V17. God placed them in the expanse of the heavens to give light on the earth,

V18. and to govern the day and the night, and to separate the light from the darkness; and God saw that it was good.

V19. There was evening and there was morning, a fourth day.

This passage denotes and defines actual sources of actual light, thereby permanently departing from the metaphor of Energy hereafter. It also denotes the first measurement of Time according to the continuation of consistent motion as governed by the Physical Laws of the Universe.

And there you have it. There is a Big Bang in the Bible, boys and girls.

good is life

Live in it or lay in it.
It's on you.

Life is what's important marching by
as we grasp numbly at what we want to believe.

How do you know the lions among men?
They act like lions.

Only the live ones dream.

Here's a little secret:

If you really are
GOOD

You don't need to be
ARROGANT

As you dance amongst life's freedoms,
be careful what you step in.
You may find to great chagrin.
that you cannot step out again.

Never use your freedom in a way that will demand it of you.

HEROES — GYROS — SCHMIROS

I'm sick of hearing it. Little secret: heroes...real ones... have very short life spans. Most of them didn't make it back...however...if you get killed in a war you are just as likely to be a hero as a fuck-up. I should know...I've fucked up many times in combat. I'm lucky to be alive. Others didn't and aren't. War is like nothing you've ever imagined. Looking at your watch for an extra ½ second could be your life's greatest mistake. I miss-judged the height of the curb and turning radius of the car I was driving, and it cost me 2-3 seconds on the "X" (the kill-zone of an ambush). It also saved my life. They thought I was going to drive forward instead of back up and the RPG went over my hood. I fucked up and it saved my life...fucking up is hit or miss, but true heroism is dangerous as fuck 24/7. When it really counts ain't enough. It's doing it every day. Because if you go in at anything less than everything, you're dead anyway. That's a no-shit hero. Like I said, most of them are dead, but a few are still around. Even then you'd never know it if you actually met one.

Don't worry.
If you're really doing really good,
it hurts a bit.

There are but few who will push the throttle forward, hard.
As far as it will go.
Just before they hit the wall:
The not to be fucked with.

You who have the right to hate,
and fight with all to keep it,
will win the prison you create,
but you will never leave it.

Tolerance is but a step from hate and miles from compassion.

THE GOSPEL OF TOLERANCE

We're all tolerating each other right now. Isn't this nice.

The gospel of tolerance is the most benign, mediocre, and pathetic standard that the human race has yet set for itself. We have all embraced it as the mantra for good and ascribed a great deal of righteousness to ourselves for adhering to its call to: "don't hate".

Yes. The message is a rallying cry to not despise each other. How empowering to each other we are! If we can but resist the overwhelming urge to strangle our fellow man, there is no end to what we can accomplish!

Well? Who the fuck even came up with that? We are tolerating the shit out of each other, and people are still in poverty! People, real people, with lives just as real as yours are literally dying because they have nothing but dirt to put in their mouths. Not hating them is just not doing the trick, God damn it. But don't get distracted. It's not about poverty. Poverty is not humanity's problem. The pain of it is. The pain of everything is.

Tolerance can't soothe the pain of anyone, no matter how much you don't care about them. Your indifference is noted. But it is not helpful. Hatred is abhorrent, but at least the object of hate has borne enough contemplation to merit a decision of sentiment. Indifference doesn't even grant its object the opportunity of inspection. Tolerance, at its very best, is the conscious decision to not think.

The gospel of tolerance, not its intent, but its actual and final product when it is played out on the stage of humanity is as unimpressively unoriginal as it is pathetic. The victims of the intolerant and of the tolerant are the same. One beats them, while the other looks away.

Men talk Jazz.
Women talk Soul.
But we each listen only
for that hint of Rock and Roll.

HOW TO REGRET

I'm glad that I did,
so that I could wish that I'd not,
otherwise, I never would have known.

THE B LINE

It will come along soon enough.
Your angst does not bring it sooner.
Your peace is yours to find or not.
But don't get on that train if you have not.
You'll never be so compelled in your life to find it.
This misery is your only chance to learn it.
If you don't you will have missed the whole lesson.

DRAGON

I'm riding this life.
I'm riding this thing like a dragon.
See, the dragon is just doing what dragons do.
And me?
I'm just hanging on for the ride.

It *is* like riding a dragon.
As if each life has a life all its own.

We meet the beast somewhere…early on.
Before time begins.
And we ride it for our life.

Some of yours are dragons like mine.
And some of yours seem doves to me.

But no.

We each ride a dragon.

Or fight it.

Or both.

Early on I know this much:
I must break it.
I must.
Or die.
Or kill us both in trying.
Better dead now from living somehow,
than dead in a life of dying.

It shrieks and roils and bucks.
And flies like fucking HATE on fire.

To break me.
It must.
Or die.
Or kill us both in trying.
Better dead now from living somehow,
than dead in a life of dying.

It is Ten-Thousand Hells of Violent Fuck
-this BEASTFIGHT lode.
Idle stands the Devil by.
Transfixed.
Somehow beaten.

But then one day in sadist taunt,
I of a sudden let it go.
To watch it try to kill me, I suppose.
I do not now sure know.

He flies like the roil of the hurriflame wind – hard, hot, mad, and
quick – like the flick of the tip of a wick with a whip – Sharp.
Violent. Perfect.

It's then, I find myself in awe of him.
My spurs and crop and beating-chains,
and all the shatter-smashed remains
of the environs where we've fought –
when he would try to scrape me off,
all hurt him. Bad.
Tough Motherfucker, I'll say that.
That's what makes him reckless and brave,
the beast knows he can take a beating.
His greatest power is in his bleeding.

Scorn bears his iron screams:
"FUCK FEAR."
"It's but the fantasy of pain," I sing.
"FUCK PAIN." He shrieks again.
"For when it's gone, I will remain." - I sing along.

I push him on. Lift him up.
And he flies even faster.
And turns ever harder still.
Like wild grace. Terrifying. Mesmerizing.
So I urge him on. With all that I am.
Then the fear: If all of me is spent to lift him up, then who is
there for me?
And the answer surges beneath me. In Power.
And I learned that when we strive in unison.
To lift the other up, it becomes a dance.
A beautiful, wild dance.
Like sex.
Striving together as one for the sake of the other.
Becoming one.
And then I knew what love is.
And then I loved myself.
Because, then I understood it: I am the dragon.

THE DRAGONRIDER'S SONG

FUCK FEAR. It's but the fantasy of pain. FUCK PAIN. When it's gone, I will remain, so long as bloody nostrils flare, and burning lungs can fill with air, the blinding shriek of soul and mind are only now. And now will soon be left behind. For only in that length and breadth of time and depth of pain is there a forge so hot to melt the dross and pure the soul and smelt and smith the mind and will to hold an edge that's sharp and hard - enough to cut the shards of dark and sheer the barbs from shattered darts stuck deep and hard in deepest parts of bloody bludgeoned soul and heart and cut the inky dungeon dark away with flame - ignites the pain - a powder keg - and sparks the conflagration through the veins and boils the blood and burns away my face erasing my identity - that others see - that wasn't really ever me and every single thing's aflame and burned away except a name and everything that isn't me has died it's gone I'm purified I'm sterile-clean, I wasn't getting weaker all along - I thought I was - but all the weight of fear and hate and pain and fake are gone away I'm strong and lean and fierce again I'm more than free, I'm less than I have ever been, I'm nothing else at all - but me.

Don't read this, Mom.

HOW TO LOVE A MAN

How to love a man she said expressionless – hidden like a treasure chest – that question is a gem – how to love a man she said again – mischievous and then it broke but she still tried to hide it. That smile she hides behind her eyes sometimes, though she knows I'll always find it. No matter where it is. It's mine. There it is. I told you so. It's beautiful. It blossoms out across the face and skin and lips and eyes and mine is there to meet it – only just the faintest brush the lightest touch is just enough to change a life to stop in time to surge the tide of life inside and find that I'm still in her eyes with nothing I can hide behind. Like summer wind the kiss begins it's sweet and slow and soft as sin the lips and neck and back and breast and then the lips again the clothes are on the grass her skin is soft her back is strong her breasts are in my face again she draws me in I feel her wet her liquid flesh her sweetest pinkest softest sin inside the wet the sex the slap and splat of cock and cunt the slurp and suck the sweat the lust the shit the fuck the look of pain the nails the veins the scraping flames her dirty gaping eyes roll back my finger finds the crack it's in her ass her vision blurs her mind explodes she shakes she squirts her face unloads emotion pain then red again her eyes are back her body tight her ass surrounds my cock it hurts at first but then she feels it deep and big and hard and pushes back I feel the surge the blood the buzz the world is red and blurred she pushes back she wants it deeper in her ass she squeezes hard she's strong as fuck I can't hold on I'm gonna cum but she's not done with me just yet – her fingers slide like lighting striking on the inside-blinding fast and deep inside my ass and blow apart my fucking mind it all goes dark I'm hard as fuck I'm blowing up I thrust again and shake a scream and quake and cum my seed erupts there's no control of anything the overload is too intense my soul's escaped to join with hers it surges through her holes and fills the temple of her soul that's hers alone on earth to give as all the holes and soul and skin of me are hers to do with as she'll please she'll play away and stay awake and lick and suck and stick her fingers in my butt and other stuff and I will do the same to her but never ever hurt the girl who trusts in me enough to let me treat her like a slut to fuck her face and butt the crazy stuff. Without the trust it's just the lust and guilt and shame and doubt and pain and all that other shit again. The girl inside of her I trust as much as I respect the boy in me who loves himself and owns his shit enough to love to lift her up above himself – it ain't just love all by itself – there's other stuff – if she actually likes the motherfucker's most of it – that's enough – it gives him fire 'cause when he looks into her eyes and sees the only thing a good man needs that she believes that he's the fucking shit - the man – the best – a beast – the God Damn Bomb – the motherfucking Virgin's womb – the goodest man she's ever seen – he won't back down from anything or any fight or any chance in all his life to prove her right and he will bend the very path of light from straight to round if that is what it takes before he ever lets himself let down the girl who treats him like her fucking man.

VAIN?

I like the shit I'm made of and how it's configured. I didn't make it, so I can't take credit or brag it up, but I sure am grateful, so I try to keep it up and take care the best I can.

I've been the outcast, the angry, weak, small, chubby kid that other guys used to pour piss on in the locker room. That was me. It never really leaves you to know that people have thought of you as less than human because at the time you are compelled to agree with them. Deep scars.

I loathe meanness, and especially true vanity: the belief that any life is more valuable than another based on the structure of matter comprising its body.

That ain't me.

We live in a BEAST.

THE BATTLE OF
THE BEAST

You must teach your beast. You cannot just tell it what to do. It will flippantly ignore you. It will get what it wants. Regardless of all the thrashing and guilt that you impose upon it. It really doesn't give a fuck about those things. And it is much stronger than you. If it thinks it needs heroine... it will get it. You are helpless against it. And if you ever fully concede your will to its strength. It will slay your will dead. With ease. All of you will become all of it. All of the best that you will only ever be, will be beast.

You secretly hate yourself because you hate what your beast does, and you think it's you. You must love yourself. Enough to seize the power to overcome your beast. You must love your beast to teach it. You cannot understand a creature that you hate and you cannot teach a creature that you do not understand.

The beast you live in is of the wildest things upon this earth. And your will alone cannot tame it. You must love it and learn it and teach it. Your beast is supremely pragmatic and supremely powerful in its element. It hates the thought of your control over it as much as you hate the thought of its control over you. And if you never tame it, you will always fight it on its terms. It will always win. The greatest strength of your greatest will is only effective against it upon your will's own battleground. The battleground of your will is Reason. You must train your beast to love what is best for it. Make it a student of the pain that gives it its most power. And it will soon understand.

Only through studied wisdom and the knowledge of its deepest desires do you have a chance. It is your very greatest enemy until you make it your very greatest friend. And no strength of mind can overcome its might... its only weakness to your will is its laziness. But that is not victory. Its strongest desires are the key. It will never want what you want unless you guide it into the understanding that what your will desires is what is best for it... for its own sake. The most strivent reaches to the human in you are the strongest against it... but never on its terms... only with supreme elegance and purpose and understanding and love toward it can you ever succeed. And then you can ride it. And it will be your greatest violence against your greatest enemies in this life.

No amount of Tony Robbins chest beating bullshit can do this. Only you can. And by your wisdom of will alone.

Because it is a wild thing. The wildest of all that is animal. For if you but let it, it has a human at its behest. Your ultimate humanity will never be realized without its brute ferocity...so when you do some day bring it 'round... in that place only, will you ever find that most wild and reckless and dangerous peace of which you've always dreamed.

LIFE AFTER DIVORCE

1 ½ oz Spiced Rum
1 ½ oz Vodka
1 ½ oz Lillet Blanc
½ oz Roses Lime juice
½ oz Simple Syrup
¼ pinch of salt

Shaken

Martini Glass

Rub twist of lemon along the rim of the glass, then drop it in.

Life after divorce - It's strong but it's sweet.

If you would that all think well of you,
you must first bear all thinking you a fool.
And after that, you won't give a fuck what any-
one thinks about you at all.
Ironic.
Anyway, that's how it works for me.
I think that's when you start to get good.

CHANGE

You fake the heat and hate the beat and blow the streets to climb the heights and fight the fights it's not the peace that pleases it's the strife and fight and grit and dirt and angst and burn to push against the wall again to feel the firm to give it all and feel it move and shift and turn and turn the throb and pulse of blood and thought and mind and bone into a fucking change.

I know for my part of only one
who keeps coming back.
Who never leaves a fallen man behind.
Who turns the other cheek when scarred.
Who lives the words that love is blind.

A friend that I have never known arrived the other day.
And though it's been eternity,
I knew them right away.

it's not the hardest part that's hard. it's all the in-betweens. the mediocrity of breathing in and out. the simple things. that make up all the rest of it. it's not the bite of life that leaves the marks. the sparks of it are part of it. but most is just the shit that happens in between the breaths of lungs and beats of heart of it.

"And those who were seen dancing were thought to be
insane by those who could not hear the music."
—Friedreich Nietzsche

This is the gospel of Jesus Christ.

You should never toot your own horn.
But you've still got to shine your own shoes.

You ALWAYS get what you want.

Relax.
Everything that you know is at least a little bit wrong.

BENJAMIN

With her hand upon the wallet – if you want call it sacrilege – she calls it what she wants – she wants it and she's calling it – swearing with her hand upon it's in my pants – it's black and big - says VISA on it – got it - got it bad – she knows I want – I love this wicked little bitch – she's sinisterly elegant - she's hot as sick is - slick as shit is – though I know her tricks I can't resist – her web is thick and always sticks – oh shit I'm stuck - she knows she's in – her only sin: she always wins - she sins and sins and sins and then she wins and wins and wins again. Tiffany's never hates – it only loves…everyone who pays and love is all you need me – say her lips – believe me – leave me be, she pouts at once, it seems that none among them leave me keys – the kind with wheels beneath – believe the heels they're leaving – loving me is easy – VISA – reaching's cute but teasing – keeping me is easy babe I'll teach you – Louis V is all you need – with keys inside – I'll pick the ride – the right apartment makes me hot it wouldn't take me long to find - cards are nice at Christmas time with diamonds in – but I'm the kind of girl that likes a card for every season, I'm just teasin', one is fine as I am, black is back and I'm the reason – can't go back you know - I thought I'd got her once she'd got the wallet out my pocket – it's a lock I'm shock and awesome – then I saw him as I opened it – oh shit it's him again – the only one she can't resist – his eyes deep green excite her dreaming mind it seems the more she gets the more he's leaving her - he always leaves his gifts behind and memories that she's got with him - sometimes he leaves her for what seems the longest time but when he's back she's his again and then immediately he leaves again in spite of it she loves him all and all that she can get of him she wants with all her life and might and might, she dreams, in time spend all her life and time with him inside her pocket - she can't help it – even gets excited when he goes, in fact, those are times she's loving him the most but hates it when he's gone again and grieving dreams she'll find a man that she can keep with lots of him, but she will always love him most because he sets her free again and gives her all she really wants but nothing that she needs it seems - he sets her free from all of them – even those that love her – all the men – the one she'll always love the most – her only love, her Benjamin.

Embrace your angst.
And you win.

She gushed with life and the things that
got in the way of it she loathed.

This is Toni Fix. The best street photographer alive today.

It Fucking Rains

ELENA'S ANGELS

Elena's angels stay awake anticipating waiting patient biding time and vying fighting for the right to make Elena's eyes light up to be the one to see the truest brightest bluest brightness all of them who've seen it say it's like the first light in the universe the day the stars ignited seared the frozen oceans' ice and vaporized it – mistified – it's like looking in her irises when she's excited flushed and smiling like the newborn atmosphere's first morning oceans form from mist and dew and quick as blush transform the hazel earth into the purest softest sharpest shades of blue – the first the angels ever knew – but angels can't persuade Elena so they watch and wait and hope and pray like me and try like hell to give her every reason she could ever think of – anything to see the blinding bluest brightness earth has ever been look me in the eyes and smile the kind of smile that makes me want to make her want to smile at me again like that and that's exactly what the danger is I'm trapped she's captivated me with all her angels facing life without parole with no control it's hopeless – let me go – unless you're ever gonna smile again and make those big bright eyes light up again and draw me in to swim in them but then I'm leaving I'm not teasing, no more tricks, that's all, that's it, I'm praying as I run away that I can make her smile again and then I'll stay – but only for a minute – this is my condition - always winnin' in this prison with Elena's angels... I guess I'll have one more round.

Mackey's' legendary bartender, Léna.

To some it's been given a map and a mark
and to own of it all they can find.
To some it's been given the sextant and stars
and but all of their footfalls behind.

"It's a bad world, Donatus, an incredibly bad world. But I have discovered in the midst of it a quiet and good people who have learned the great secret of life. They have found a joy and wisdom which is a thousand times better than any of the pleasures of our sinful life. They are despised and persecuted, but they care not. They are masters of their souls. They have overcome the world. These people, Donatus, are Christians... and I am one of them."

—Cyprian

Stolen

Build your boat.
Not the river.

The loudest voice is seldom wisest.

March 19, 2019

I wasn't going to, but I finally opened the cheap Moscato and drank some. It was almost 11 after all. Another flat and dull morning that seems to call to me to write it down beautifully, but I can't seem to get myself out of the way. Plus, just writing down the morning doesn't do it justice because there's no human experience in it. Being a writer in Africa was so much more romantic. There I was, a burgeoning writer risking it all. Here I'm just a dumbass who can't hold a full-time job because of his pesky writing compulsion. Oh, but I wish it were that strong! I'd love for my art to be so strong as to derail everything. As it is, I've derailed everything to make room for my art. I hope it works.

My only real passion is drinking before noon.

It seems like I can't write as well now because I have fewer doubts about God to write about.
What a son-of a-bitch problem to have.

I live a meager yet soulful existence.
As a businessman it's shit.
But as a writer, it's not bad at all.
I rather like it.

The Bar Buzz makes me want to write. I love the feel of it. The noise and the rubbing of humanity on itself. I love that. It's not really necessary to drink to observe it but it's a must if you want to participate in it. And if you don't, then you get the feeling that you should really just get the fuck out.

I have $8.

Getting some beer gut but not past saving with some fasting and some juice.

Good thing for me it's 2 for $8 for Yosemite Roads wine at 7Eleven.

My $8 with some coins out of my change bag was enough for a couple bottles.

He couldn't write a word, so he sat there in the wine bar by himself. It was empty except for him and a bottle of Bordeaux that he was drinking fast enough to give away the fact that he was trying to get drunk. It was good. A nice smokey rich roll after the initial pucker telling you that it's French.

March 27, 2019

I had done it.
I was finally drunk.
Oh the sweet relief.
From what?
From whatever.
From whatever scares me when I get too high.
It can always get worse. Always.
But there's not really much outside of abject poverty and home-
lessness left to worry about.
Most of the bad shit has already happened to me.
At least once. Even that.
I feel kinda bad about it. I shouldn't be drunk at 10 AM.
Lots of people would say, nawwww, don't worry about it.
I wouldn't like most of them.
Most of them are just looking for someone else to be as fucked
up as they are.
I am.
But the world is full of drunks so who's to know what the general
consensus is on anyone's right to get drunk.
I figure I've a right if anybody does.
Even says in the Book "Give strong drink to him who is perishing,
and wine to him whose life is bitter. Let him drink and forget
his poverty and remember his trouble no more."
I'm down.
So I'm just going to keep hangin' on to that bit of license until
the last I can.

I'm stuck in this lukewarm melancholy.

How the hell am I supposed to write from here?

I'm terrified of the terror of the pressure to write that will come upon me when life gets really bad, but that's just how it works sometimes.

All the time for me it seems.

I wish I could write without the pressure.

Without the terror.

I hope I can, but it seems to me that I'm far too far out of hell to write and I have no desire to go back there.

But oh to ring those words from the angst.

Not the words so much as the authenticity.

That's what I'm after, God damn it.

I'm pissed I'm not tortured, but like a hound who's been beaten, I'm gun-shy as hell.

What the hell am I absorbed with?

Can I write good happy shit?

Is the deepest form of communication through pain?

Probably.

It's the only thing that all of humanity can relate to.

Writing like a madman digging for the water.

The road to death is littered by the words of shitty poets.
It's like double hell.

Hey, what's your name pretty girl?
I can't say that I care.
That's not true.
I think you're beautiful.
I just don't give enough of a fuck to go through all the bullshit
it would take to convince you that I'm not like all the limp dick
assholes that you've dated before.

People always want something from you.
People who would con me soon learn that I ain't got shit.
People leave me pretty well alone.

It's drunk here.
I'm 3 a.m.

I wish it was more.
But I'm getting there.

One by one the ideas and lines parade through my brain.
Drink makes them better I think.

I pick and choose. Kill, kill, kill, keep, kill, tweak, kill, kill…
That's all it is. That's the grand secret.

Usually you kill most of it. Or all, but sometimes you can keep
a lot.
That's when it's really going good.

That's when you've found your natural point of aim.
That hasn't happened in a very long time,
but it's nice when it does.

Usually it's a hard bitter grind full of doubt
Then somehow at the end of it,
If you make it that far,
It's a poem.

That people won't read in their normal condition.

Bukowski, you motherfucker.

The muse has left, it's for the best, there's booze to drink and weed to smoke and I'll pretend until the end that I don't give a damn. But I do, it's no use, I can't find a rhyme to save my fucking life. I can't find a beat to save my fucking heart. I'll be afraid and walk for miles and pace about inside my room, but in the end my best and only pen will come through for me. I'll write again someday about something important. And until then my only friend will be the end of this bottle, joint, and block.

A HEART THAT I
CAN FIGHT BESIDE

It's just another bullet – leave it be, so she can pull it – a couple bullets more is all I need to get me home to keep me going – I left most of mine behind in hearts and minds it's hot it hurts it's sharp but light the burning tells me I'm alive it keeps me running through the night that's satin black and grainy green and flashing white sometimes – red dots - red eyes like mine behind the sights – one each is fine my ammunition's running dry as I am fighting's gotten tiring dying's gotten easy as my trigger squeeze is – a thousand miles or so I hope but I don't know how far she is or where or who or when I'll finally find her – finally put my hand behind her waist and hold her hand in mine and dance in spite of all the lightning - gliding finally safe inside a heart that's kind but fierce but soft but scarred but brave like mine – a heart that I can fight beside.

for my Lila who found me instead

THE PACK

Pack and pack and pack and pack the pain is in my lower back but we keep packing never waiting, only ever hesitating when the damned chutes drop in and only if and only when we're done with all that's on the floor and after that we pack some more, the only way to make it stop is sweating harder bigger drops upon the wretched parachutes, fucked and flipped through, lines a-shit, kill line probably fucking ripped and rubber bands all broke to fuck, "we need two more before the bird goes up", the god damn team loads never end until the day is done my friend, it's six-six-six, the devil's number, eighteen tandems, four damned packers, two of us are turning two on every load except the new guys, turning one and shitting bricks and sucking on a bag of dicks, because they ain't had any break all day, they're too damned slow to beat the loads and then the people want to talk and ask them questions while they pack: When do you replace the rubber bands? How come the airplane always lands before the chutes, and on and on and all the screams and Whoops of joy like salt rubbed in the fucking wound.

for the pack at Skydive Snohomish

SHIT

I only sense that the punisher's there.
And that crime and the sentence are written somewhere.
I feel like I'm drowning in shit.
Cat-scratching the bounds and the filth of this pit.
It's like someone is closing it - rubbing my nose in it,
piling the rocks on the lid.
I'm fucked as a felon
despite my rebellion
I slipped, and I tripped, and I fell into hell and
I don't even know what I did.
And now I'm consigned to the grind.
Condemned to the walls of their miniature minds,
and defined by the shit under my fingertips,
that I peddle as if it were mine.
Hooray for the peddlers of shit.
And Hooray for consumers who eat all of it.
And chained to the oar with the damned and the poor,
are the minds who would live by their wit.

The drab grey and gloom all around,
it quickens my eyes to what brightness I've found.
And the shit peddlers droning and spewing their lines,
makes my heart long to speak only in rhymes.
It's all that life isn't that's starkest and clearest.
The beauty that's missing is my sweetest nearness.
And searching in vain, I suddenly find
the beauty I seek taking form in my mind.
The ominous weight that smothers my will,
also sharpens my mind and quickens my quill.
It's that dull heavy burden again and again,
that crushes me squeezing the words from this pen.
Go into the darkness as deep as you dare.
There only you'll find the diamonds.
In the blackness of earth where the pressure is worst
is the only place you will find them.
The poet's hell is the sunshine.
No gold is found in the flowers.
Look in your despair - you'll find treasure there,
in the depth of your desperate hours.

It's a lot less about knowing what you ought to do,
and a lot more about doing what you know you ought.

Everyone is always saying that your life will get better.
It will.
Tremendously so.
But ONLY if you take tremendous risk.
Aversion to it is the greatest recipe
for despair and a shit-ass life.

Art is the purest projection of the fiercest form of yourself.

You will never overcome life's greatest obstacles.
Those, you must transcend.

SO, BREATHE

If only I could walk, I would only run.
If only I could speak, I would only sing.
If only I could feel, I would only love.
If only I could think, I would only dream.
If only I could hear, I would only listen.
If only I could see, I would only seek.
If only I could have all I'm only missing,
I would only live, if I could only breathe.
So, breathe.

I find it interesting that the best things usually go unseen.
The worst things are out in the open and loud
for all to see and begging for attention.
But the best things are the silent things.
And I do believe there are many, many more of them.

Not of the Supernatural is God's most remarkable work,
but of the Ubernatural.

The direst of our deepest desires is rooted, not in finding the position and capacity to receive love from another, but rather to find the person willing to receive all the love which we are so deeply driven to give.

Do you really think that the truth is so exclusive that you are the only one who knows it? It's much more likely that some other SOB is closer than you and you are one of the fools that you condescend to who you see stumbling around in their own absurdity. I'd say it's much more likely that the absolute truth is both clear as day in front of your face as something you have already rejected, yet somehow in its entirety, incomprehensible. But then again, I'm just one more of the stumbling fools.

The greatest enemy of great success is success.

Whether for ass or truth,
you must grope with empty hands.

Did you see the early church attacking others in any way?
Ever?
No.
That trait was Roman.
Then the church thereof.
Then of its splinters.

Sensation is the enemy of action.

I love being a man. I don't love being a man because it's easy. I don't know any kind of man that loves that life. He's a goddamn pussy. I love being a man because it's really fucking hard and in the hardest ways. And you keep your goddamn mouth shut. And you don't bitch about it. And just get it the fuck done. The best way that you can. And that's being a man.

Life don't owe you shit.
You owe you shit.

The science of beauty is art.

Life costs you everything in the end.
What are you saving it all up for?
Spend it wise but spend it all.

MURDERER OF YOUR OWN SOUL

We are all entitled to a certain measure of it. Not one of us is safe. For we each dole it out, and every person, color, and creed suffers it. The dismissal of this fact neglects history, reality, and the wherewithal to comprehend either.

But here's the thing about it... it will strangle you in the warm and easy soak of assurance that it is well deserved. And it's true. It is.

But it does not matter how legitimately entitled to it you may be. Revisited, it intensifies its only butcherous obsessions : guile and sabotage.

As you seek and find and claim every right to all of it that you merit, its appetite is commensurately increased. Its bitterness conjures new instances from a past of its own manufacture. It skews the history that once belonged to you that it may feed and live and grow upon its own irresistible contrivances.

It will, in time, kill all of you but the stale beat of your lifeless heart. And the only surviving freedoms left to the authentic self of your will, are to escape the plodding monotony of the flow of blood through your veins, or madness, or the languishing palpitation in each insipid thump of the dead thing in your chest until the end of your wasted life.

It is not hate. I led you wrong there. Hate is but one of many vigilant guards of your walls and bars and chains: your only defense against the siege of life.

And these champions, at your behest, sanction but a single and venerated and constant companion: the only thing you cling to close enough to shove the blade in slow enough for you to feel all of the pain most, without notice.

The murderer of your own soul is your own pain.

Abdication of your legitimate right to it is your only hope. For when you free it from your cage, so will you be.

But you alone must confront its most stalwart guardan: Yourself.

As previously published in *The Boise Beat.*

There is only one thing that separates the writer, the actor, the painter, or singer from an Artist: Courage.

All the religions of the world are in different ways, the discovery of the truest potential of the tremendous capacity of the most amazing creature ever created by the only thing that can ever save them from their fucked-up position in eternity.

Poetry is not dead.
Poets are.

You must grope blind alone along the
bottom grime for the good stuff.

Here's to you Chris Kempner. Keep shining.

You can't just STOP failure or success.
It's not a rope.
It's a part of the ocean.
The rope is truth.

"The good that you do in this world is for all
of humanity. The evil is for yourself."
—Elihu

Do you really think that the truth will be popular?
What name makes you most uncomfortable?
Buddha
Muhammad
Krishna
Jesus Christ

Yet still now, any reason to scorn Jesus
of Nazareth remains unfound.

I will always treat you like a brother.
It's all I've ever had.
So, I don't know any other way.
I will always and forever do all and everything I can ever imagine
to do for you...
And I will always talk straight with no bullshit.
So, if that works...
I'm good at it.
My brothers have taught me how.

For Fats and Beano

The really good stuff is just beyond the really hard stuff.

BECOMING ALIVE

The most essential ingredient of a lame-ass life is comfort. It's the God of this nation. You worship what you most fear living without. The thirst for it is insatiable, its power domineering, its devastation perfect... and its carnage utterly indiscernible. It will kill who you most deeply long to be and you won't even know it happened. And you never will. Because... it's comfortable. It's its own poison.

Hungry. That's what "slender" feels like.
Exhausted. That's what "proud parents" feels like.
Painful. That's what "awesome" feels like.

There's some damn fool notion that if you're really doing really well, you're comfortable. Complete bullshit. When you get to the base of the mountain. The one that's really worth climbing. And you're looking up at its peak. You're going to realize something: you aren't strong enough to make it to the top. And you'll be right. But you who will start to climb in spite of it... you will soon discover the secret: the only way that you can ever become strong enough to climb to the top of the mountain is by climbing to the top of the mountain. You will be strong enough to make it to the top in the instant you arrive there.

It's called "becoming". And becoming just sucks. It is supposed to. If it doesn't, you aren't. And the more it does, the more you are... but only if you get to the end. Because if you stop in the middle of it... you will die there.

It's a good thing we don't remember our own birth. We were supremely comfortable in the womb. Then without warning we were plunged into the most horrifying and painful experience of our lives. And at the end of it we took our first breath of life. We would have preferred to stay in the womb. Had we done so, we would have died. And had we not undergone the entirety of birth's anguish, we would have died. Our only chance at any of life was all of the angst of becoming alive. Nothing has changed.

As previously published in *The Boise Beat*.
Here's to you, Ed Simon. Thank you.

The only way to heal all the pain is to feel all the pain.

Thanks for teaching me this, Krystle.
Thanks for showing me this, Eddie.

"I have seen something like it happen in battle. A man was coming at me, I at him. To kill. Then came a sudden great gust of wind that wrapped our cloaks over our swords and almost over our eyes, so that we could do nothing to one another but must fight the wind itself. And that ridiculous contention, so foreign to the business we were on, set us both laughing, face to face – friends for a moment – and then at once enemies again and forever." -C.S. Lewis

The wind is the sword of Truth.
It renders each our own ridiculous.
It can't not win.

DON'T NOT THINK, God Damn it.

Don't cut God any slack. He hates that shit. Either let Him be God or nothing at all. Ask Him to show you who He is, and if He doesn't, then don't fucking believe in Him.

RULE #1: Don't be a pussy.

Stolen from Troy Conrey.
I'd bust you out of a Chinese prison any day, brother.

David, Dani, and Ryker:

There is nothing on this earth you cannot get once you realize there's nothing else on it that you really want. Hunt and kill your lesser wants, for they alone can kill your greatest.

You are my life's greatest experience and joy.

Be strong and courageous... especially in how you think.

I am always loving you.

—Dad

The dark is finally fading into grey - it seems the light and truth are hating it away and things are stark and clean and marked with things I haven't seen in years – since last I saw the day – like hope and open air and light – besides the lighting strikes – something's under the horizon rising slight – too slow to notice – but I know that I remember how to see – it's not just hope – I know what light is – with last drop of blood and strength and life that's left in me - the bars of darkness slowly start to bend - it seems I may have somehow been redeemed - the night just might be finally coming to an end.

Jason Lee Morrison